CONTENTS

INTRODUCTION

In the age of addiction to excitement and celebrity, many teach us to flow in the gifts of the spirit, but few show us how to demonstrate prophetic character. Carrying a mantle and a mandate comes with stress and trauma. Persecution is the inheritance of anyone who walks in the ancient office of the Prophet; therefore, the prophetic lifestyle is about more than issuing forth the Word of the Lord.

You can look at any area of the life of those who are mature prophets and see the Word of the Lord. Their lives are consumed by the passion and zeal of the Christ. Even the example of how they handle their weaknesses is a prophetic instruction to us all. Their lives are a word. The Western church is filled with prolific illustrations of Sunday morning glory; few, however, have been willing to carry the mantle into Monday actualization.

Many apostles and prophets have been stuck going around in circles because they don't know how to govern what they've been given. For each mantle, a particular attitude, disposition, pain tolerance, and flexibility level is required. Prophets of God need to know that they are more than their gift. Many of us in ministry have relied on our calling to be our source of praise and affirmation. Yet when we live by the praise of men, we will die by their critiques.

One of my greatest concerns as I look at my generation is that we won't have the longevity required to fulfill our assignments. We've been graced by God with a degree of discernment that surpasses our ordinary life experience.

The ease of access to revelation has deceived many into thinking that they've arrived at special places in the spirit that they don't have the discipline or character to maintain. One of my constant meditations is to understand that I need God more and more each day because a great start doesn't always guarantee a phenomenal finish.

As we look at the prophetic generals of the generations before us, we can learn many lessons about how some stayed true to their responsibilities, and how others missed the mark and ended their work prematurely.

The most dangerous blindspot in this current prophetic flow is not false prophecy, but a loss of emphasis on the cross. Training in our giftings has been more important than ensuring that prophetic voices are focused on the evangelistic assignment that all believers have, the great commission to "make disciples" of Christ.

If Jesus is not the focus, the prophetic has no point. Calling names and laying hands on people in services where people are "slain in the spirit" means nothing if our eyes are not fixed on the Son of God. The rise of the New Age movement is creeping into the apostolic and prophetic streams. In the African-American church, both the Black Hebrew Israelites and a demonic call to return to the so-called gods of the "motherland" are capturing people right and left. A prophetic response is required to the demonic doctrines consuming the hearts of men and women all over the world.

These New Age and spiritualist movements demote the Christ and promote supernatural access without the cross. In Luke 4, Satan offered Jesus the ability to rule and reign without his having to go to the cross. Satan tried to tempt Jesus with premature acceleration into another phase of his calling. But Jesus knew that a crossless path was a counterfeit road that would merit nothing; so he remained steadfast.

The devil is trying to play the same trick on *us*. He is trying to give power, leadership, and spiritual authority without the trauma and discipline associated with bearing a cross. These crossless movements are compelling people whose hunger for temporal elevation and supernatural ability outweighs their desire for God.

If those speaking with a prophetic voice do not have their eyes on Jesus, their efforts are without merit. By subtle leading of the Spirit of God, I've written this book to do nothing more than to remind God's prophets to keep their eyes on Jesus so that the outcome of their labors will be in proper order.

The prophets of God have much work to do at this critical hour. We cannot handle the grave challenges in front of us effectively if our eyes are more on our giftings than on the cross. For this reason, many in my generation struggle with consistency and longevity because our gifts don't take the cross for us. Only when a prophet has his eyes aimed toward the Son of God can he or she truly see.

The problems and flaws that we perceive in ourselves aren't the ones hurting us.
The issues that we can't detect are the shortcomings killing us slowly. God has truths that He wants to deliver to us, but the messages don't come through when we're too preoccupied with our gift.

Once we begin to look at Jesus, we can see how distant we are from him. We begin to see how deficient we are, yet how perfect he is. The more we discover his beauty, the more our character will transform to match his. Christ has been on the backburner of the prophetic movement for too long. It's time for the prophets to arise and center our vision on the Son of God.

BLINDED BY YOUR INHERITANCE

Our familial environment is the first educational institution that we attend. Our caregivers are our first examples. They train us in communication, conflict resolution, stewardship, diet, and everything else we need to know. Our family is the initial resource we have for learning anything. We inherit both their vision and the blindspots that accompany their sight. When God needs to call a prophet out of the bondage of an inherited blindness, He demands separation.

Now the Lord said to Abram, "Go from your country and your kindred and your father's house to the land that I will show you. 2 And I will make of you a great nation, and I will bless you and make your name great, so that you will be a blessing. 3 I will bless those who bless you, and him who dishonors you I will curse, and in you all the families of the earth shall be blessed." -Genesis 12:1-3

Rabbinic tradition holds that Abraham's father, Terah was an idolater. God had a plan to bless the whole earth through Abraham's life, so He had to sanctify him by separating him from what he knew. God couldn't allow Terah's vision to corrupt what He wanted to show Abraham.

God promised Abraham to multiply his seed as the stars of heaven. If Abraham had taken Terah with him or lived according to the cultural conditioning of his home, he might have been convinced that the Lord wasn't the one speaking to him, but rather, the sun, the moon, or the stars. The gods we bow to determine our level of sight and clarity.

Many prophets can't arrive at their promised land because they've allowed the voice of family idols to convince them out of the plan of God. When God is grooming prophetic voices to rise above the idols of the time and proclaim the way of the Most High, He has to detach His servants from the limitations that originally trained them. Without some form of separation from our origins, we can have no vision.

Whether you're rich or poor, you inherit your worldview from the context of your upbringing. Some of us come from two parent homes where we were never celebrated, so we gravitated to destructive behavior as a means to receive attention. Others of us grew up in poverty with a single parent who was under the influence of an addiction.

With that as our background, we had to grow up faster than everyone else because we were raising both our siblings and our parents—and ourselves.

Everyone has a unique story. Our earliest pains shaped how we interact with people now, how we define success, and how we've structured our emotional and psychological needs. We were trained in habits and disciplines that may or may not be currently beneficial to us. We've been given a lot of weaknesses by way of where we came from.

Many of us have been trained to believe that the best way to deal with a weakness is to pretend that it doesn't exist. That's why many prophetic people live double lives. They're powerful with a microphone, but suicidal when they're alone. The glory of God hits when they lay hands on people, but they can't stop themselves from laying hands in the bedroom on people who aren't their spouses.

One of the dangers of living a double life is that you slowly begin to disassociate yourself from reality. You say to yourself, "I don't need to ask for help. I can stop anytime. Everybody's got something to deal with." The question is, are we aiming to live like everybody or like Christ?

We have to be real with God about where we are. He can't help the person we're pretending to be; He can only heal the person we actually are. A doctor can't diagnose us if we never confess that anything is wrong. He can only move and prescribe a solution according to our word. If we're not honest, we can't receive help.

Jesus, of course, knows more than our doctors. He can tell if we're pretending. We have to confess the truth of what's going on with us if we want his help. He's not going to force his way through our pride. We must humble ourselves and approach him from our genuine position.

But some of us have been pretending for so long that we've lost touch with who we are in fact. We've forgotten what's really true. The worst situation to deal with is to be blind and not know it. Jesus rebuked the Laodecian church because they were the same way, in a state of self-deception.

"For you say, I am rich, I have prospered, and I need nothing, not realizing that you are wretched, pitiable, poor, blind, and naked." -Revelation 3:17

Healing mandates we admit we have a problem that requires his attention.
Many of us walk and talk as if we're whole, but we're broken. We preach as though everything is fine, but we're in pain.

We head to work like we're not dibbling and dabbling, but we're popping pills to sustain ourselves through the days. We lead our families with care, but keep a bottle of Hennessy in the closet. Making ourselves up to look one way and yet living another seems an easy route to follow. The Bible calls it having the form of godliness, but denying the power.

The church may have mastered the form, but we need God's very real presence in spirit. The more we ignore our issues, the further we bury them. If we live life pretending everything is fine, we won't approach Jesus in the way that we need to.

35 As he drew near to Jericho, a blind man was sitting by the roadside begging. 36 And hearing a crowd going by, he inquired what this meant. 37 They told him, "Jesus of Nazareth is passing by." 38 And he cried out, "Jesus, Son of David, have mercy on me!" 39 And those who were in front rebuked him, telling him to be silent. But he cried out all the more, "Son of David, have mercy on me!" 40 And Jesus stopped and commanded him to be brought to him. And when he came near, he asked him, 41 "What do you want me to do for you?" He said, "Lord, let me recover my sight." 42 And Jesus said to him, "Recover your sight; your faith has made you well." 43 And immediately he recovered his sight and followed him, glorifying God. And all the people, when they saw it, gave praise to God.

The urgency of our felt need determines the volume of our cry for help. If we're used to pretending, we'll see Help walking by, but we won't say anything. The blind man at Jericho didn't care who saw him or heard him. They tried to shut him up, but he didn't care about holding onto his reputation. He cared about his deliverance.

When deliverance is a greater priority than our image, Jesus will set us free. We should approach God not with our titles and degrees, but with the depth of our desperation. We should come to Jesus with a cry that shakes the world around us. There are prophets who refuse to go to the altar because they're concerned about their image. When we see Jesus passing by, we must cry out because we don't know when our next chance will be.

Whether we're living in sin or not, I believe that praying from our blindness is our wisest move. A regular prayer of mine is "Lord give me the wisdom I need for today. I've never been in today before, but you have. Open my eyes so that I can see what you see." When we approach God as if we know it all, we prevent ourselves from learning what He sees.

God is glorified when He takes weak and blind men and women and gives them grace to receive His vision. Jesus doesn't want to use only your strengths to gain some glory, he wants to use your weaknesses as well. He wants to use your blindness to show the world that He can make anyone see.

Whether helping with a familial trouble or any other type of struggle, God has a plan to take the issue that you inherited and win the glory from it. If you're honest about where you are, He will take you to where He is. We earn longevity in confessing our weaknesses to acknowledge His strength. If His strength is made perfect in our weakness, that means what we couldn't do in our own power, He can do through us in His.

We are all born with numerous blindspots. We can see several examples of our visual limitations by way of human anatomy. No way can I see if I have a spot on the back of my shirt. Seeing what's going on inside my stomach after eating is impossible. I may have no clue if something's stuck between my teeth or obnoxiously dangling from my nose. We're born with a measure of limitation. Our Pharisee-like religious culture has taught us that blindness and limitations are of the devil. But a realm of blindness has been encoded in our DNA. If we don't embrace the fact that many things we cannot see, we'll never pursue the Jesus who opens blinded eyes.

BLINDED BY YOUR PATH

When God calls us to do something, he often requires us to do it under cover of darkness. He told Abram to leave his family and go to a land that he hadn't seen before. He told Joseph that his family would bow to him and then sent him down to a dark pit. Saul, who became Paul, was struck with a bright light that made him blind.

The human eye can barely handle the brightness of the sun, so how much more difficult is it to encounter the brightness of Christ. The light of Christ shines in such a way that we can't avoid damaging our retinas. In the great spiritual adventure of our lives, we must walk by faith and not by sight if we're to progress. If we were to ramble along with the great men and women of scripture, we could see that many of them began their encounters with God in darkness and uncertainty.

As he passed by, he saw a man blind from birth. 2 And his disciples asked him, "Rabbi, who sinned, this man or his parents, that he was born blind?" 3 Jesus an-

swered, "It was not that this man sinned, or his parents, but that the works of God might be displayed in him. 4 We must work the works of him who sent me while it is day; night is coming, when no one can work. 5 As long as I am in the world, I am the light of the world." 6 Having said these things, he spit on the ground and made mud with the saliva. Then he anointed the man's eyes with the mud 7 and said to him, "Go, wash in the pool of Siloam" (which means Sent). So he went and washed and came back seeing. -John 9:1-7

The painful life of the prophet can be riddled with questions. Why me? Why this way? Why this attack? Why this circumstance? We're eager for answers that give us vision and clarity, but the truth is, God allows some blindness in life so that his glory can be revealed.

In John 9, Jesus lets his disciples know that neither the man nor his parents did anything to cause the man to be born blind. His blindness came so that God's glory could be revealed. God preordained a specific time for this man to be healed so that He could display His power and authority even over His genetic code.

God births our prophetic destiny in blindness so we will learn early on to depend on Him. If we were able to complete our assignment in our own strength and understanding, we wouldn't need God. Many of God's prophets feel confused when they suffer stress, difficulty, and discomfort, but this is the inheritance of the prophetic office. The blindness of a seer is where their sight lies. The office of the prophet ultimately thrives under persecution, pressure, and distress.

Even some of the greats were driven into depression when they couldn't see their way to the future. One of the greatest pet peeves of a prophet is to not be able to see. Jeremiah the Prophet was arrested by Pashur the priest because he released a word of judgment. After being beaten and put in the stocks, Jeremiah uttered some of his most oft-repeated words, about there being a "burning fire" shut up in his bones.

The prophet didn't say this because he was shouting or doing a victory lap. He was laying out his complaint before the Lord. He was angry because the things that he was prophesying were getting him into trouble, and whenever he felt like giving up on God, something came upon him and burned him to prophecy. He felt that God was using his strength to bully him in life.

The man of God was frustrated because he could see the destiny of the people, but his own destiny seemed to be uncertain. God hadn't revealed the full picture to him, and yet eventually the prophet pressed forward. The attitude of a prophet is one of obedience and dependence. God expects us to live by faith day by day and moment by moment. Prophets must have total trust in God because they

—and we—can only see as far as Christ wants us to see.

Many of God's prophets today have been given microphones before they've been given time to learn to have total dependence on God. The maturity of a prophetic voice is not merely in the accuracy of the gifting, but more so in the ability to be led in darkness. God speaks to us in pieces and glimpses. He allows us to see parts of the whole. One major hindrance to deeper revelation is disobedience to the last instruction.

Some people of God are frequently stopped from discerning either in certain areas or on the whole because they're too busy being frustrated by what they can't see and can't know. The frustration blocks them from following through on what they do know. We don't jump from sixth grade to twelfth grade in a day. We are taught lesson by lesson, and once we prove proficiency in the content of a grade, we can move onto the next level.

Some students refuse to progress because they don't like their teacher's style. They fuss and complain and neglect to turn in homework because they believe the work is too hard or they don't think the teacher has a good attitude.

When the case comes to our Heavenly Father, we often act like ungrateful, disruptive students. He tries to show us the way lesson by lesson, and we refuse to give Him our best effort, yet we then blame Him for our underperformance.

The path that we're called to requires that we follow God's turn-by-turn directions. If God gave us all the instructions at one time, we wouldn't be able to comprehend His directives, let alone be able to follow. Some directions don't make any sense until particular points in the journey.

Maturity for a prophet of God is about being able to go with the flow of divine disruption. Prophets have to be okay with knowing the end from the beginning, but still have to walk through the unmarked pathway in the middle.

The greatest prophet, Jesus Christ, the Son of God and sole purpose for prophetic ministry, gives us the best example of how to be a prophet in the middle of destiny.

23 And when he got into the boat, his disciples followed him. 24 And behold, there arose a great storm on the sea, so that the boat was being swamped by the waves; but he was asleep. 25 And they went and woke him, saying, "Save us, Lord; we are perishing." 26 And he said to them, "Why are you afraid, O you of little faith?" Then he rose and rebuked the winds and the sea, and there was a great calm. 27 And the men marveled, saying, "What sort of man is this, that even winds and sea obey him?" -Matthew 8:23-27

When a man or woman of God is in the middle of a storm they should be resting. When uncertainty abounds, we should be patiently waiting on the Lord. We should have a Christ-like peace because we know who has authority over the sea.

Jesus didn't bother to comfort the disciples because to Jesus the storm was normal, a simple part of his journey to the other side. He rebuked his disciples for their lack of faith. In his correction, he juxtaposed their faith with their fear, implying that the presence of fear comes down to the absence of great faith.

The disciples lived through the lens of their limited experiences. All they knew was that powerful storms on the sea kill men in boats. Their vision taught them that men can't conquer storms that large.

Jesus knew that he had authority over anything that would try to overtake him. Instead of saying, "Father how could you let a storm of such proportions come near me," he stayed comfortably asleep. He knew that storms were natural and he had the authority to impose his supernatural understanding over the natural. Jesus was living according to what he could not see, while the disciples were living solely according to what they could see.

Jesus had a breadth of vision that enabled him to

walk on the plane of higher level laws, allowing him to calm the greatest tempest. For example, the law of gravity is certainly true: What goes up must come down. But higher laws of aerodynamics learned only recently in man's history permit airplanes and other aerial machinery to circumvent the law of gravity. Prophets that walk by faith and not be sight, live by higher level laws.

Jesus walked in a totally different realm of reality because of his level of clarity. The level of vision that prophets walk in determines the laws of reality that govern their lives. The disciples knew that natural laws dictated the odds as being against them.

They had every right to fear and imagine their demise. They had an excuse to worry, to be depressed, and to be anxious. They had an excuse to curse Jesus out because of the situation. Natural excuses remove us from the supernatural workings of God.

Christ's example here emphasizes that a prophetic life is one lived in total faith and dependence upon God. We can't speak to storms that we can't sleep through. We can't command wind and waves to cease in other people's lives if we're afraid of them in our own. Dependence is key if we are to have proper vision.

God's prophets must learn the lessons of true vision, which has to do with seeing a problem from God's perspective. We must be okay with resting in the midst of storms if we're to see earth-shattering prophetic revival in the land.

BLINDED BY YOUR MOTIVES

Despite what the reports may be, I believe the church is in an extraordinary age of its rich history. God has poured out a multitude of fresh streams of revelation. People in and out of the pulpit have the power to bubble forth world-changing truths at the drop of a dime. The revival of the prophetic and apostolic offices in recent years has helped us to move deeper into the knowledge of our Lord and Savior Jesus Christ.

Revelation, knowledge, and insight are everywhere. The advent of digital technology has expanded our ability to share and impart knowledge, experience, and wisdom. While the world is becoming more wicked, we ought to pay attention to how God is giving us further profound comprehension and revelation to navigate the difficulties that this hour demands.

However, the cliche "with great power comes great responsibility" rings true. In the blink of an eye, a person can step out of their lane and become a Bible teacher or prophet when doing a live video on social media. People can post insights online that God ordained only for personal consumption.

People who have not been assigned to preach or teach on a public platform are literally running full-time ministries online based on receivings that God never intended for them to share. Many of these individuals are led by the intoxication of likes, hearts, and other forms of social engagement (which has been engineered by tech companies to be addictive) rather than the Holy Spirit.

Given the ease of access to a carnal public forum, people are entering into ministry without the call of God and pursuing advancement for selfish and fleshly motivations. Jesus is no longer the star of the show. The church has placed Christ on the back-burner while wondering why some churches and denominations aren't seeing miracles anymore.

We have stepped into a time in which the majority of the members in prophetic and apostolic houses want to conduct full-time ministry. Many of us have abandoned the call to win the lust due to a lust to be famous in church.

People are writing blogs and books and producing live videos on Christian topics simply because they see the church an easy market to crack into. God has little to do with a significant portion of the content written and posted about Him these days.

Jesus has become the symbol to fund our dreams and aspirations for not working a nine-to-five job and for having a flexible schedule. The American church in particular is inundated with ministers and ministries that operate for personal gain rather than for the advancement of the Kingdom.

When we have improper motives, they eventually become buried under our activities. We see people who are successful in what God called them to do, and we say to ourselves that we want what they have. We see the lights and the stage and the theatrics of ministry while not discerning the will of God. We have a moment in which we see what we wish we could be, and we start carrying out activities that will propel us to the position in which we see that other person. We tell ourselves our conduct is for souls or for the Kingdom, but deep down, many of us minister to cope with our painful self-esteem issues.

The more actions we take with a bad motive, the deeper we bury our initial intentions. Eventually, we forget that we preach because we like when people tell us that we're amazing. We prophesy because we love the rush we feel when the crowd looks at us. I've heard more than one man of God from the older generation warn me not to ever become one of the prophets who "loves the crowd, but hates the people."

Once we've blinded ourselves to our true motivations, God can still use us, but we have difficulty growing in relationship with Him. Just because we're developing in the prophetic and thriving in ministry doesn't mean that we're flourishing in our relationship with Jesus.

Jesus in Mathew 7:22. "On that day many will say to me, 'Lord, Lord, did we not prophesy in your name, and cast out demons in your name, and do many mighty works in your name?'" God can use us to do mighty works, despite our poor motives, but that doesn't imply that we're in an intimate fellowship with him.

The devil loves for people to become drunk on their increase in the gifts of the Spirit, but remain completely oblivious to their lack of an intimate bond with the Lord. Your gift is a vehicle for the voice of God for others. Many people can hear God only from their gifting because they actually have a weak relationship with him. So they can only receive the teachings that the gift can deliver. Just because God is speaking to us in the stream of our gifting doesn't mean that He's speaking to us intimately.

Sometimes my wife and I text about bills and financial matters to make sure we're on the same page. In those iMessage conversations, we exchange pertinent information, but if our relationship were solely based on texting about bills, our marriage would be in serious trouble. Our intimacy is much more powerful when we're having in-person conversations about things other than money.

Some of us are only hearing God when He needs to use us. He can only get our attention when a bill is due in the spirit or when we have some person to minister to or some emergency to handle. We have put up a wall of distance between us and the Holy Spirit, otherwise. The veil keeps us from seeing how close and affectionate Jesus truly wants to be with us.

God didn't create Adam for ministry. He created him for sonship. His assignment came as a consequence of his relationship. Just as He created Adam, God made us to walk with Him in the cool of the day. Before we come to serve as prophet, apostle, bishop, pastor, or anything else, we are God's children. God wants to renew the son in you.

We must "minister" to Him first, so that He can constantly give us His vision and His heart. David wasn't a man seeking God's wonder-working power, but His heart. Because David pursued God's heart, he flowed in a prophetic anointing that foretold the arrival of the Messiah. Thousands of years after David's death, the church hinges on the comfort, encouragement, and revelation of his words. When we open our eyes to the heart of God, there is nothing He won't reveal to us.

In prayer, we exchange our heart for His heart.
Our motives for His motives.
Our pain for His pain.
Our desires for His desires.
Our blindness for His vision.

BLINDED
BY YOUR
UNIQUENESS

He was a man of power and demonstration. He was a prophet of both activity and accuracy. At his command, the meteorological systems of the earth stalled. The Lord listened to his voice and raised the dead. He was an antagonist to the demonic agenda and had an appetite to glorify God and destroy the works of the devil.

At the height of Elijah's career, he sent fire from Heaven in a duel that one would assume to have been of epic proportions. The prophets of Baal versus a sole Prophet of Yaweh. The stage was set for a contest far greater than Ali versus Frazier. King Ahab had sent for all the people of Israel to be front and center to see which god was true.

This produced a great show, but not much competition. The prophets of the Canaanite deity gave their all, but their god was silent. The prophets of

Baal cried out from morning until noon, but they received no answer. They began cutting themselves in the hope of getting Baal's attention.

Elijah confidently mocked the prophets of Baal and proceeded to show the Lord to be the true and living God. After his prayer, a fire came from Heaven that consumed his offering. This was a day when people saw the manifestation of God's power right before their eyes.

Elijah had just won a mighty victory over his chief adversaries with the entire nation looking at him. The king and queen felt threatened. What could they say against such a mighty sign? How could they explain Baal's inability to make even a peep? The hearts of the people were with the God of Heaven and his Prophet.

In the kingdom of darkness, I believe they have a motto: "When in doubt, intimidate your way out." King Ahab and Queen Jezebel were powerless against a man who called down fire from Heaven, but they were fine as long as Elijah didn't realize their weakness. Sometimes, the greatest threats are no more than fear disguising itself as confidence.

Jezebel began by sending a threat to Elijah that broke him to the core. She threatened to kill Elijah by the same time the next day, and the mighty prophet of God immediately spiraled into a depression. He asked the Lord to kill him as he slept away his sorrow under a juniper tree.

If we believe the lies that intimidation brings to us, we'll be too blind to see how much power God has given us. In less than a day, Elijah went from calling fire down from Heaven to sleeping under a tree in despair.

The enemy knows that he can't take the power away from a true prophet. All he can really do is play mind games to make prophets forget about God's power. Elijah was so focused on the enemy's power that he lost sight of God's supremacy. Elijah paid attention to the threats of demons rather than the promises of God, whom he lived for.

There are many prophetic people in mental crisis. They have a word and assignment, but they also have enemies. They follow the voice of God, but they also respond to the voices of their enemies. We can see a level of prophetic schizophrenia on the earth right now. Countless prophets are elated by major victories on Sunday, but asking God to take their lives on Monday.

We may ask, how is it that they could be blinded so quickly? Why are God's people losing focus? They want to believe, but what's holding them back? I believe the answer can be found as we continue to journey through the history of this mighty prophet of God.

Elijah has a conversation with God in 1 Kings 19 that reveals the core of his fears. He tells God, "For the people of Israel have forsaken your covenant, thrown down your altars, and killed your prophets with the sword, and I, even I only, am left, and they seek my life, to take it away."

Whenever someone of political or religious influence wants control, they can't tolerate God speaking so they shut up the prophets, at all costs. Some duct-tape the prophets, while others, like Jezebel, kill them. The queen had a great track record of killing God's prophets. The prophets who once traveled together and learned together were now buried together.

This would be an intense and emotionally draining season for any prophet. Your friends, colleagues, confidants, and sons—here today and gone tomorrow. Death became commonplace for the men who held the breath of the God of life in their mouths in Jezebel's day.

Elijah had seen a lot of prophets die. This period was a time in which that's what he knew and experienced. So when Jezebel told him that he was next, he believed her. Sometimes, we can begin to believe life's experiences more than the God who created life itself.

Elijah thought that he was the last man standing. He

thought he was the only one left living right. Every season of life brings tests, troubles, and trials. As we progress, we often leave people behind who don't want to continue into the future. They have a public fall or private failing, and they don't recover. We see decay and decline all around us, and as we continue to press forward, the bodies that Jezebel sends lying in the streets begin to haunt us as we recognize how rare we are. As we envision the days to come, we have flashbacks of the last prophet we had to bury.

Some of us see so much death and so little life that like Elijah, we believe we're the only ones living right. We are ultimately haunted by our uniqueness. In our circle, we may be the only ones pressing for more of God. We may be an anomaly in righteous living and we feel as if no one else is left.

That day, God let his prophet know, you're special, but not that special. In 1 Kings 18:18 the Lord said to Elijah, "Yet I will leave seven thousand in Israel, all the knees that have not bowed to Baal, and every mouth that has not kissed him."

When we focus on how unique we are and how rare we are, can't see Jesus. As Peter the Apostle walked on water, he began to look at the winds and the waves instead of the Christ. The more we reflect on how difficult the mission is, the less we will consider the cross.

A constant focus on our rarity can cause us to think

that we must obey God out of our own strength. The weight and pressure of what God has called us to do becomes too heavy to handle. From that point, we begin to rely more on our intellect and our resources rather than on God.

Once we realize that our intellect, resources, connections, skills, and abilities are not enough for the task at hand, we crash, because we weren't meant to fulfill our prophetic purpose without God. If we could defeat Ahab and Jezebel without the Holy Ghost and his power, that wouldn't be our assignment. God only gives us callings that require His support, because the purpose of life is to come to know Him.

Everything God gives us to do is bigger than us. If we focus on what we know and how difficult and rigorous our undertaking is, we will crumble under the weight of the call of God.

Our uniqueness becomes a liability when we lose touch with who made us. In Elijah's mind: *All the other prophets are gone, so what makes me think I can escape her claws? They were living for God. They were obeying him, and they fell. How can I be so special to avoid calamity?*

Eventually, the thing that separates us from the crowd must make us realize that we're just like everyone else. We have to realize that we need the same blood and we're alive by the same grace of

God. When a prophet comes to depend on God, he will have longevity. Elijah's successor, Elisha, comes to the fore because of the prophet's petition for death in a place of depression. Elisha was God's response to Elijah's prayers.

We can only wonder if Elijah and Elisha could have done more, had Elijah won the war in his mind. This is merely my conjecture. How many prophets have to release their successors prematurely because they're unable to handle the psychological warfare associated with their charge? When we keep our eyes on matters that intimidate us, we will be blind to the reality of the Lordship of Jesus Christ.

He is Lord over what we understand and what we don't understand. He is Lord over what we know and what we don't know. He is Lord over what we see and what we can't see. Neither the Jezebels nor the Ahabs of our given tasks can stand in the way of the weight of his glory and majesty.

BLINDED BY YOUR SUCCESS

On more than one occasion, I've wept in church. Sometimes, I'm repenting with my head down before God in the midst of a convicting message. Other times, I have my hands lifted high in praise because of the goodness of God.

And still other times, I weep because I look around in a service and I see all the empty seats. I am convicted because I know that more people out there need to hear what God is saying. Every empty chair reminds me of the body of Christ not coming to terms with who we really are. Every empty chair reminds me that we have more work to do. I ask the Lord how I can improve. How we can be better.

Much of the body of Christ has become so comfortable with the degree of God we have that we're not concerned with how much of God the rest of the world needs. We have a plethora of people in our families, schools, and workplaces we haven't shared the gospel with. We've become so comfortable being around the walking dead that we don't think to speak the word of life.

Leaders, prophets, and churches often arrive in success and hit a plateau when the infectious hunger that brought us to achievement begins to fade away. Our churches aren't growing because we've become content with where we are.

Sometimes, the greatest hindrance to progress is past success. Subconsciously, we feel that we don't need to see more souls in our churches because we feel good about how many we currently have.

One time, the Lord rebuked me and said, "You can't see the greatness that I have for you because you've gotten comfortable with the good that you've already arrived at." This conversation isn't limited to evangelism and church growth. It pertains to every area of our lives.

The biggest barrier to making more money is how much money you're currently making. The greatest obstacle to a great marriage is a good one. God's prophets have been at ease living with 3.0 GPAs in the school of life because they're doing better than the average. Others are just fine with mediocrity.

Some of us testify so much about past miracles and victories that we've deceived ourselves into believing that we're still on that same level. In actuality, we've receded because we feel comfortable with the last miracle God used us to perform.

One of the dangers of success is that if we're not careful, achievement will rob our hunger while we're not looking. Prior accomplishment can seduce us out of having a vision for the future.

Not only must we press forward toward God faithfully to unlock his desire for the next season, we must stay hungry for the Lord so that we can maintain what he's released to us. Many have been so centered on achieving that they forget the importance of maintenance.

Once that longing for a triumph has been satisfied, we may fall prey to a temptation to let go of all the discipline and passion required to obtain a promise from God. The deception is that we're still moving forward, even though the victory is in the past.

The passive approach to maintaining what God has given leads to mismanagement. Neglect is a crippling form of mismanagement because the blindspot doesn't lift until what we're taking care of dies. The Failure reveals that we weren't paying attention.

Some people ignore the oil light on their cars for months at a time. They believe that just because the car is working, everything is fine. Once the engine is blown, they begin to truly see how careless they've been.

The energy and time they invested in researching the car and securing the right loan should then have been transferred to routine maintenance to ensure continued use of the vehicle.

Many prophets are walking the earth with blown engines. The victory of the accomplishment is overshadowed by the necessity for proper care. We can see evidence of prophetic neglect with how many tasks remain undone throughout the earth right now.

We have a class of believers, however, who give their all both before and after major triumphs, but they still walk in a dimension of blindness. One assumption that many of us make is that our success implies that we're effective.

I remember working for a particular organization that has several offices in all fifty states. The group managed millions of dollars and served several thousand customers. The company sat at the top of its industry. After working there for a bit, I knew its success couldn't last forever.

Management's approach to solving problems was from the 1960s, and the technology infrastructure there was severely outdated. If the firm's executives had begun their work in the modern era, they would never have been able to get off the ground. To their advantage, they had capital amassed from being in business for over one hundred years.

As time passed, other companies began to outpace them and now the company is seriously considering bankruptcy. Although the business was successful, the executives didn't realize that they were tolerating the company's underperformance. The blindness of ineffectiveness blocked them from seeing the threats to their success and opportunities for improvement.

We can all probably point to many everyday examples of giants being undermined by what's in the blindspot. Blockbuster missed the mark on Netflix. The taxi industry has had to massively give way to Uber. Myspace let a kid in a college dorm outpace them.

The complacent are at the mercy of the disruptors. Just because we've obtained some level of success doesn't mean that we don't have more to grasp. When organizations refuse to evolve, they refuse to survive.

Non-evolving organizations are the product of non-evolving people. Many of us are growing in revelation and knowledge but not using what we learn to evolve. When we don't transform, everything that we're responsible for stagnates.

Could it be that churches are doing, because prophets are growing stale? Could it be that regions and nations are perishing because the prophets of God refuse to grow?

Hunger is the driving force of innovation. If we feel no hunger, we won't look for what will work next and prepare for what's ahead. The hungry are inventive and solution oriented.

Hunger drives us past obstacles and thrusts us into progress and peak performance. The earth is diluted with underperforming prophets who believe their gifting is good enough to guarantee them the future that God showed them. The future is for the hungry.

BLINDED BY HYPOCRISY

King David sat on his throne in a strange place. He didn't seem fazed by what he had just done. Once a sweet, innocent shepherd boy, he had been jaded by the pressures and the pains of kingly rule. He was fatigued from the emotional and psychological effects of warfare. In the spring when he was supposed to return to battle, a woman by the name of Bathesheba had caught his eye.

He was supposed to be fighting, but he found himself resting with a woman that didn't belong to him. With his political authority he coerced Bathsheeba into his chambers and having her one time wasn't good enough.

He hatched a murderous conspiracy to make sure she would never reunite with her husband, and that the baby on the way from his moment of indiscretion would be shielded from reproach.

King David seemed unmoved by what he had done. So God, in His mercy, sent one of His best on a mission to rebuke the king.

The Lord sent Nathan to David. When Nathan came to the king, he said, "There were two men in a certain town, one rich and the other poor. 2 The rich man had a very large number of sheep and cattle, 3 but the poor man had nothing except one little ewe lamb he had bought. He raised it, and it grew up with him and his children. It shared his food, drank from his cup and even slept in his arms. It was like a daughter to him. 4 "Now a traveler came to the rich man, but the rich man refrained from taking one of his own sheep or cattle to prepare a meal for the traveler who had come to him. Instead, he took the ewe lamb that belonged to the poor man and prepared it for the one who had come to him." 5 David burned with anger against the man and said to Nathan, "As surely as the Lord lives, the man who did this must die! 6 He must pay for that lamb four times over, because he did such a thing and had no pity." 7 Then Nathan said to David, "You are the man!" -2 Samuel 12:1-7

David couldn't tell that Nathan was talking about him. His heart was in such a hardened place that God had to use a character in a parable as an example to show him his behavior. As we walk in the prophetic, God shows us many things about people. We dream dreams and have visions. We're filled with revelation regarding where people are missing the mark. One of the dangers here is that our spiritual perceptions can blind us to our own personal character flaws. We can be so busy perceiving what's going on with others, that we ignore the Holy Spirit when He checks us.

One of the understandings that prophetic people need is that even when God is talking about "them" he's always dealing with us. What if what God keeps showing you about other people is really a lesson he's trying to get you to see about you. When God shows you that someone is living in fornication, he has also encoded a warning for you not to do the same thing. What we see for others can speak similarly to us.

It's not about him.
It's not about her.
It not about them.
It's not about it.
It's all about you.
Thou art the man.

In Luke 12, Jesus warned us vehemently against disassociating ourselves from what we preach.

In the meantime, when so many thousands of the people had gathered together that they were trampling one another, he began to say to his disciples first, "Beware of the leaven of the Pharisees, which is hypocrisy." -Luke 12:1

I find it interesting that while Jesus is before a crowd of many thousands, he turned to his dozen first and began to teach them. Before God can deal with his sheep, He has to reach the shepherds. As prophets, we have an obligation to first have our ears tuned to God for his personal warnings, admonitions, and rebukes.

Jesus lets his team know that hypocrisy, like leaven,

starts out small but spreads quickly. Hypocrisy is the blinding force that blocked the Pharisees from receiving Jesus as Lord.

The Pharisees loved to find fault with others, but could never see anything wrong with themselves. In Luke 11, Jesus gives seven woes to the Pharisees because of their hypocritical worldview and perspective on the scripture. Hypocrisy is often the birthing place of a dead religious spirit because with it we can find a fault in someone, but lack the compassion and power necessary to bring deliverance.

A lot of prophets use their gift to condemn and criticize others instead of imparting, building, and training. Prophets must be cautious not to become *pharisitic* parasites that spread the leaven of hypocrisy. We can unwittingly use our sense of privilege from the Lord as an excuse to walk in suspicion and pride.

We can become so intoxicated delivering messages to "them" that we never allow what God is saying to work within us. I've seen a lot of prophetic Moses types in the land who can lead people into promises that they'll never be able to cross over into themselves.

If we don't become the primary recipients of the revelation God gives us, we will watch the people being blessed while we stand and wonder why God isn't moving for us. Furthermore, when people have trouble understanding what God is saying or need help applying revelation, we'll have no real experiential context to answer their questions.

Many of the prophetic leaders have become like fitness trainers who are gluttonous and obese. They have a bunch of knowledge and revelation that they haven't applied, but insist on teaching others.

God told the Prophet Ezekiel "...Son of man, all my words that I shall speak to you receive in your heart, and hear with your ears" (Ezekiel 3:10). The words of prophecy that we take in, we first receive in our hearts and hear with our ears. Ezekiel couldn't effectively prophecy against idolatry, greed, and corruption if he was practicing those sins. We must give people food that we're willing to eat ourselves.

9 So I went to the angel and told him to give me the little scroll. And he said to me, "Take and eat it; it will make your stomach bitter, but in your mouth it will be sweet as honey." 10 And I took the little scroll from the hand of the angel and ate it. It was sweet as honey in my mouth, but when I had eaten it my stomach was made bitter. 11 And I was told, "You must again prophesy about many peoples and nations and languages and kings." -Revelation 10:9-10

In Revelation 10, John has to eat a scroll that is sweet to the taste, but difficult on the stomach. When we serve to others what we're unwilling to eat ourselves we become a graceless and proud people.

We lack grace because we remember the sweet taste of the revelation, but forget the bitter feeling of when God's Word settles on the inside and rips our insides apart to make us more like Christ.

A graceless prophetic culture is the antithesis of what Christ died for. 1 Peter 5:5 lets us know that "God resists the proud, but gives grace to the humble." We don't always feel good when God is getting rid of our pride, rejection, anger, fear, or lust. Sometimes the dealings of God are very bitter. Many of us are circumcising people in prophetic, yet we're unwilling to be held accountable to the knives of our own leaders.

Hypocrisy makes us feel that we're okay when we compare ourselves to other people. The problem is that we're supposed to use Jesus as our measuring stick, not other people.

When prophets don't move in the grace of God, they will rightly discern the flaws of others, while erroneously passing judgement on them. Once God shows the prophets something about someone, their first response is to condemn the weak instead of interceding for them. The gifts of the Spirit aren't everything. Sometimes God shows us surface level information in the spirit about others so that we can go and ask them how we can help. Judgement is God's job, not our own.

Hypocrisy causes us to see people according to their flaws more than their purpose, calling, and identity in Christ. With pride, we judge people in reference to labels and suspicions that we have and call it the Holy Ghost. We have become a people who can't see a weakness without being judgmental.

By the grace of God, we want people to move to Jesus and away from sin and condemnation, but a hypocritical prophetic voice lusts for the judgment of God. The prideful prophet will proceed to live out the wrong example in the parable of the Pharisee and the tax collector.

Two men went up into the temple to pray, one a Pharisee and the other a tax collector. 11 The Pharisee, standing by himself, prayed thus: "God, I thank you that I am not like other men, extortioners, unjust, adulterers, or even like this tax collector. 12 I fast twice a week; I give tithes of all that I get." 13 But the tax collector, standing far off, would not even lift up his eyes to heaven, but beat his breast, saying, "God, be merciful to me, a sinner!" 14 I tell you, this man went down to his house justified, rather than the other. For everyone who exalts himself will be humbled, but the one who humbles himself will be exalted. -Luke 18:10-14

Graceless ministers like to see the judgment of God in the lives of others because the judgement gives them fuel to justify their own sense of entitlement and self-righteousness. Like the Pharisee, they say,

"I am not like other men. I don't club, I don't drink, I don't smoke—so my own righteousness makes me right before God."

The error is that our righteousness is not good enough to justify us before God. As Isaiah said, our righteousness is as filthy rags. We may not be drinking and smoking as we used to, but I sure know a lot of prophets who procrastinate when God speaks.

I know a lot of men and women of God who don't sleep around or do drugs anymore, but they're in bed with laziness and addicted to the drug of inconsistency. When God looks at righteousness, he views the whole picture. Many prophets of God have stopped cursing, but they walk in gluttony daily. They're led by their appetites and haven't turned down their plates in years.

We all need the grace of God, because of the many assignments that we've omitted. If we want judgment for "them," then we're also requesting judgment for ourselves.

When God judges, he doesn't overlook the sins that we think are small. They're all the same to him. If we approach God in our own righteousness, then we reject the grace to approach him boldly through the righteousness of Christ.

When no grace is to be found in a prophetic atmosphere, the gifts of the spirit are misused, mishandled, and abused. Where there is no grace, the word of knowledge becomes the word of pride. The discernment of spirits becomes the discernment of personal suspicions. Prophecy becomes the gift of judgment and condemnation. So called prophetic gifts become tools for our adversary and accuser.

Legalistic culture interferes with our discernment because Christ is not at the center of a people living according to law and judgment. A lust for judgment is an artifact of a people bound by the Mosaic law. A passion for mercy is the mark of a people who walk in the grace of Christ. As we make Jesus our focus under his grace, the sin that has kept people bound will have no choice but to fall off. Hypocrisy blinds us, not just from accurate discernment, but from the One we should have our attention on at all times, Jesus Christ.

Eddie Ezekiel Massey III

Scripture quotations are from the ESV® Bible (The Holy Bible, English Standard Version®), copyright © 2001 by Crossway Bibles, a publishing ministry of Good News Publishers. Used by
permission. All rights reserved.

www.ingramcontent.com/pod-product-compliance
Lightning Source LLC
Chambersburg PA
CBHW020438030426
42337CB00014B/1312